D1598122

ST. THOMAS
ON THE OBJECT
OF GEOMETRY

The Aquinas Lecture, 1953

ST. THOMAS
ON THE OBJECT
OF GEOMETRY

Under the Auspices of the Aristotelian Society
of Marquette University

BY

VINCENT EDWARD SMITH, Ph.D.

MARQUETTE UNIVERSITY PRESS
MILWAUKEE
1954

Prefatory

The Aristotelian Society of Marquette University each year invites a scholar to deliver a lecture in honor of St. Thomas Aquinas. Customarily delivered on the Sunday nearest March 7, the feast day of the Society's patron saint, these lectures are called the Aquinas lectures.

In 1953 the Society had the pleasure of recording the lecture of Vincent E. Smith, Ph.D., professor of philosophy at Notre Dame University. Dr. Smith was educated at Xavier University in Cincinnati; the University of Fribourg, Switzerland; Institutum Divi Thomae, Cincinnati; Harvard University, and the Massachusetts Institute of Technology. He received his Ph.D. degree from the Catholic University of America where he taught from 1946 to 1948. He has been on the philosophy faculty at Notre Dame since 1950.

During World War II he was a radar engineer in the U.S. Navy and received a commendation from Fleet Admiral Nimitz for developmental work in radar counter measures. After the war he served with the U.S. Naval Technical Mission in Europe.

Dr. Smith has been editor of *The New Scholasticism*, the journal of the American Catholic Philosophical Association, since 1948.

He is the author of the following books: *Philosophical Frontiers*, Catholic University Press, 1947; *Idea-Men of Today*, Bruce, Milwaukee, 1950; *Philosophical Physics*, Harper and Bros., 1950; *Footnotes for the Atom*, Bruce, Milwaukee, 1951.

He is also the author of numerous articles which have appeared in scientific and philosophic journals of Europe and the United States.

To the list of his writings the Aristotelian Society has the honor of adding *St. Thomas on the Object of Geometry*.

ST. THOMAS
ON THE OBJECT
OF GEOMETRY

St. Thomas on the
Object of Geometry

MATHEMATICAL knowledge has always been haunted by ambiguity and is the easiest, among human sciences, to be carried to extremes. Science and art, liberal and practical, inductive and deductive, the work of both the intellect and the imagination, mathematics is akin to logic, physics, and metaphysics and has at various times impersonated each of them. Hovering between physical and metaphysical knowledge, it affects the whole order of human sciences when its object[1] is deformed, and among the lessons of modern thought is the power of mathematics to pass for other sciences and its impotence to reconstruct a single one of them.

The nature of geometry is one of the

great classical problems in philosophy, worth re-stating in any age because the answer contains truth for every age. It is tempting to hold on the one hand that a material thing is only geometrical or, on the other, that geometry has nothing to do with reality at all. What is the abstraction peculiar to mathematics? What is the quantified being so abstracted and re-garded not simply as quantified but as being? What is the continuum specifically envisioned by geometry? This combination of questions can turn the lock to reveal the object of geometrical science, but like all questions, they must first be properly raised before they can be effectively solved. Our quest for the object of geometry will have three stages: the nature of mathematical abstraction; an analysis of quantified being first in terms of being and then in terms of quantity; and finally the problem of the continuum.

In the spectrum of present-day philosophy, there are two extreme views about the nature of geometry. On the one hand, there is the over-empirical view, encouraged by Einstein,[2] where geometry descends into a branch of physics and submits to experimental test. On the other hand, there is the over-formal view of Hilbert, Russell, and the logical empiricists, where mathematics is raised into a kind of logic.[3] Within that wide sweep of present-day opinion, a third possible position, that of Pythagoras and Plato, is no longer visible. Yet from the case argued by Aristotle against this Pythagorean-Platonic view and continued, clarified, and completed by St. Thomas Aquinas, there is much to be learned about the object of geometry and the bond between geometry and the real.

Geometry is one of the two distinct species in the genus of mathematical sciences.[4] It studies continuous quantity, like lines, planes, and solids, while arithmetic is the science of discrete quantity, like number. Between geometry and arith-

metic, there are various mixed sciences,
but there is no distinct science of quantity
as such apart from its character as continuous or discrete.[5] To study quantity as
an accident related to substance belongs to
metaphysics, and to metaphysics, as the
ruling science of philosophy, belongs the
hard subterranean work of charting out
the object of geometry.

If geometry is a science, it must demonstrate, and demonstration, like all syllo-
gisms, is a movement of the mind from
principles to conclusions. Before demonstrating, however, whether in geometry or
in any other science, the mind must ac-
quire, by way of determination, the causes
and principles that make demonstration
possible.[6] In the first two books of the
Physics, for instance, there is not a single
demonstration but only this pre-demon-
strative quest for the principles and causes
from which genuine scientific knowledge
can issue. Both in determining principle
and in demonstrating conclusions, man

must work from what is more knowable to him toward what is more knowable in its own nature, and in general, what is better known to us, like the sense world, stands lowest in the rank of absolute intelligibility, and what is more intelligible in itself is the least intelligible to us, like God as studied in natural theology.[7]

In approaching the object of geometry, it must be pointed out that the cleavage between what is knowable in itself and what is knowable to us is not always the lot of human science. Throughout the whole of mathematics, as St. Thomas sees it, what is better known to us and what is more knowable in its nature always coincide.[8] A triangle, as a three-sided figure, is more knowable both in itself and with respect to us than its familiar property of having 180° as the sum of its interior angles. St. Thomas, the philosopher, concedes even more to the mathematician. Because mathematics does not require a vast fund of experience in the learner, it

can be taught to the young, and in the
ideal pedagogical order, it comes first
among the sciences of the real world.[9]
Furthermore, because of its method of pro-
ceeding from one thing to its properties
rather than, as in the study of nature, from
one thing to another thing, mathematical
knowledge is the easiest and most certain
of human sciences.[10] And finally, because
the mind remembers what is well ar-
ranged, the striking order in mathematical
knowledge allows mathematics not only to
be the first scientific habit to be acquired
but the hardest to forget.[11]

But such a vision of mathematics by
St. Thomas creates an apparently serious
challenge to his whole theory of knowledge. Is he not on record that the philosophy of nature, not mathematics, is the re-
gion of science most configured to the human intellect?[12] And has he not reported
that the proper object of the human mind
is the "quiddity or nature existing in corporeal matter,"[13] the *quod quid est* com-

mon to all substances and accidents?[14] How can such views, describing the natural object of the intellect as the substantial or accidental quiddity of sensible matter, square up against the notions that mathematics transports the mind to closest and even coincident touch with a scientific object and that the mathematical sciences are the easiest to learn and the most certain to possess and the most difficult to lose?

The response can be formed out of the rich distinction between determination, where the mind seeks causes and principles, and demonstration, where the mind reasons from those causes and principles it has previously determined. What is more knowable in itself and what is more knowable to us do coincide in the mathematical order but only at the level of demonstration, as in the case of the triangle whose properties are to be deduced. In the order of determination, there is no such overlap between what is well known to us and better known in itself, and here the mind must make its normal curve from effects toward causes and principles. Thus, a solid is better known to us than a plane, a plane than a line, and a line than a point.[15] In other words, the point, a principle in the science of geometry, is known only after a resolution from what is more familiar to us. Because this determining process takes its rise from the changing, sense world of experience, the philosophy of nature remains the science directly tailored to our way of knowing, and it is studied after mathematics so that the learner may in the meantime enlarge his experience for a more fruitful scientific analysis of nature later on.

In any science, there is a descent from universal first principles and causes toward more particular conclusions and effects, and the philosopher of nature, at work in a world proportioned to the human tools of knowing, begins by abstracting the most general principles within this sensible universe where man is now at home.[16] The object of our science of nature exists in the material world and is studied by reference to this existence.[17] The philosopher of nature traffics in sensible matter, the world of place and time, of light and shadow, of sound and taste and touch, the world of coming to be and passing away. In nature, coal is identified by its color, sugar by its taste, a dog by its bark, cotton by its softness—and by all other characteristics of such things that the senses can reach. Nowhere does the philosopher of nature put the sense world behind him. He cannot of course articulate his science in terms of individual things, and hence as in every science, he abstracts the universal; he makes his scientific report not about this lump of coal or that grain of sugar but about coal in general, sugar in general; his object is envisioned apart from individual sensible matter but not apart from universal sensible matter.[18] In brief, the philosopher of nature remains wholly within the mobile world that first salutes our senses, and he simply begins his science by travelling within that world to the first and universal principles, like matter and form, which apply to all else within it.

By contrast to the sensible matter which occupies the philosophy of nature, the object of mathematics does not exist in the way it is studied, or rather it is not studied in the way it exists. In the mathematical order, besides the universalizing abstraction common to all scientific transactions and alone needed to get the philosophy of nature under way, a peculiar abstraction of another sort must first liberate the mathematical object. Mathematical science is required to abstract the general from the particular because it is science; it is required to make a second and special kind of abstraction because it is mathematics.[19] Such a distinctive mathematical abstraction is termed by St. Thomas the abstraction of a form.[20]

In the literal translation of St. Thomas'

language, two capital claims are made for mathematical knowledge. First of all, mathematics abstracts, and secondly, what is abstracted is form. With respect to the first point, mathematics takes its rise from that sense world which is the matrix for all the ideas ever accessible to human science;[21] indeed, in the sanely realistic vision of St. Thomas, mathematical ideas originate by induction and from the experience of particular things.[22] If this is true, then the mathematical object is drawn somehow from the world of experience; and by contrast to the postulational method of the formalists who allow mathematics to take any arbitrary starting-points, provided only they be consistent, complete, and mutually independent, St. Thomas anchors the principles of mathematics firmly in the sense particulars. He assigns no adjective to the term abstraction. He does not say that mathematical reality is known by analogy to sensible things or in that *via negativa* by which the mind envisions the object of metaphysics.[23] There is, for St. Thomas, no double movement, comprising first an abstraction and then an idealizing of the abstracted object. Whatever it may later come to mean, there is in mathematics a pure and simple abstraction.

St. Thomas maintains in the second place that mathematics abstracts a form. By contrast to the over-empirical approach to geometry, there is a vision in mathematics not of the whole physical order but of a certain part of it which may be called a form. But what is this form which makes mathematics mathematical and forbids it to pose as a physics on the one hand or a logic on the other? Is it substantial form, accidental form, or possibly neither of these? If quantity follows upon the matter of the mobile world, by what right does the mathematical object belong to the order of form?

From one point of view, the form abstracted in geometry is certainly that of an accident—the dimensions and figures and other terminations of quantity,[24] and St. Thomas does not hesitate in the proper context to contrast the accidental form studied in geometry with the substantial form that cannot be abstracted from sensible matter.[25] That of course would be the first and simplest answer that would greet our quest for the object of geometry. Such an object is simply accidental form. But there is much more to the geometrical object than this and much more subtlety to the notion of mathematical form, and to discover what it means to abstract a form from matter in geometry is not an easy task.

To begin with, the abstraction of *man* from individual men is a physical abstraction of a whole from its parts, yielding to the mind an object in the philosophy of nature; to abstract *circle* from bronze is to abstract a form from matter and thus to reach an object in geometry.[26] In clear contrast to the philosophy of nature, mathematics does not envision even common sensible matter.[27] If the circumference of a circle, being a line, has no thickness, it cannot be seen or touched; a circle makes no noise and can neither be smelled nor tasted. Moreover, it has no principle of motion within it, and if it be imagined to be moved from one place to another or to grow or diminish in size, this is, literally, only an imaginary motion. For the circle, larger or smaller in size, or in a different place, is no longer the same old circle but a new one that is different from the first. A circle derives its identity from the points terminating a radius, and the imaginary change of one or both points simply yields a new circle, leaving the old one as immobile as the two points that immobilely specify it. There is no reference to real place in mathematics,[28] and mathematical objects have no potency[29] for a new place or for any other new form. They cannot be generated or corrupted, augmented or diminished, changed in quality or in location. Our circle would truly look to be beyond the moving, sensible universe, and one is tempted, like Plato, to assign it to another world because it seems too spiritual to be in matter.

And yet a circle is more than pure matterless form. It is material in some way because extended. Part of it is here and part of it there. It has size and shape, a center and a boundary, an inside and an outside. The accidental form terminates a subject without which it could neither be nor be conceived. In the words of St. Thomas, the terminations of quantity, which are accidental forms, "cannot be considered without understanding the substance which is subject to the quantity, for that would be to abstract them from common intelligible matter. Yet they can be considered apart from this or that substance, and this is to abstract them from individual intelligible matter."[30] Such is the common teaching of St. Thomas, but when we come to analyze intelligible matter in our quest for the meaning of form in mathematics, the difficulties of finding the nature of the geometrical object as a form only mount and multiply.

If substance, as subject of quantity, is intelligible matter and if intelligible matter is envisioned by mathematical abstraction, then the form attained in geometry cannot be merely accidental form but somehow involves what is substantial. Yet if the mathematician somehow attains to substance, he would seem to gain a more profound insight into reality than the philosopher of nature; and because substance in the material world is not a form but a composite, the notion of the form abstracted in geometry seems more obscure than ever.

In an analysis that eventually casts light not only on the meaning of geometrical form but on the ultimate realism of mathematical abstraction itself, St. Thomas argues that material substance receives its accidents in a certain order of natural priority and posteriority. The first accident of matter is quantity, then comes sensible quality inhering in the substance through the medium of quantity, and finally the actions and passions of the moving world. Without quantity spreading them part after part, sensible qualities would collapse into indivisible points that could no more be seen and touched than the geometrical point with its lack of positive extension.

Now if the qualities in the material world require quantity for their sensible nature, they cannot be grasped without quantity; but since quantity is prior to sensible qualities, quantity can be considered without considering such qualities. To take an example from a different but perhaps more illuminating area, *animal* in man can be understood without reference to the rational, but *rational,* in the sense of discursive reason, cannot be understood without animal. What depends for reality on another thing depends on it also to be understood, and what does not depend on another thing for its being does not depend on it for its understanding. That is why a genuine science can abstract, and yet be fully in touch with reality. In any composite, the mind can consider one feature without considering the others, provided that what is considered does not depend for its being on the others. Although the mind cannot consider *poet*, without considering *man*, it can consider *man*, without considering *poet*.

Pressing on this logic, it can be said that substance does not depend on quantity either to exist or to be understood, but quantity depends in both ways on substance. It is this substance, as subject of quantity, that St. Thomas terms intelligible matter, and in such a view, mathematics, although relinquishing sense qualities from its consideration, does not leave aside substance from its scientific object.[31]

Yet all of this analysis, while possibly furthering our search for the meaning of geometrical form, only aggravates the

problem of the distinctive character of geometry among our sciences. Indeed, it
would look as though mathematics edges
deeper toward the roots of the real world
than the philosopher of nature, who leaves
the treatment of substance to metaphysics.[32] Plato and Descartes, not Aristotle and Aquinas, would seem to be right
after all, if quantity has a real priority of
nature over the sense qualities studied in
the physical order of knowledge, and the
hierarchy of the sciences would seem to
follow, at least at this point, a similar hierarchy in the real world. In fact, both Aristotle and Aquinas are agreed that the physical is related to the mathematical by way
of addition, since the nature adds mobility
to magnitude.[33] What is mathematically
impossible is therefore physically impossible but not vice versa. Frequently, in
the philosophy of nature, Aristotle intro-
duces a mathematical absurdity to settle
a physical argument, but he cannot intro-
duce the physically absurd to disprove a

mathematical argument. Does this mean
that mathematics takes us farther into matter than the philosophy of nature?

To allay this argument, it should be
kept in mind that nature exists in order to
operate and that the final cause is the most
explanatory instrument of human science,
since it is a *causa causarum*.[34] Now in the
hierarchy of substance plus quantity plus
sensible quality, it will be seen that the
motions of matter, last in structural analysis of nature, are first in operational im-
portance.[35] To use a technical term, the
qualities and motions of matter are first in
intention but last in natural execution. It
is only when we know the end of a thing
that we fully know it.[36] It is only through
knowledge of the qualities and motions,
which follow quantity in the order of gen-
eration and for which quantity prepares,
that we know even why quantity in the
physical world is structured into this form
or figure. Hence, while quantity lies closer
to substance than quality and while diver-

sity of figure reveals diversity of substance for our intrinsic definitions,[37] quality and motion which are as ends with respect to the quantity of things yield a deeper vision of our sense world. Hence, the philosopher of nature, in pursuit of the *causa causarum,* actually cuts deeper into the physical world than mathematics. It is significant that Descartes, who turned nature into a mathematical affair, loaded his projects by ignoring genuine final causality in his physics. In the three-stage structure of substance plus quantity plus sensible quality, mathematics does not go farther than the philosopher of nature. Stopping with only the first two members of the hierarchy, it does not go as far.

Does this mean that the mind begins with substance and then goes on to consider quantity and finally sense qualities? Or does the human mind work the other way, considering first quality, then quantity, and finally substance? Actually, in the analysis of St. Thomas, the order from substance through quantity to quality does not reflect the order of learning but rather the order of the objective structure in things themselves and a defense of the realism of mathematics. Such an analysis explains how the mathematician, when leaving aside sense qualities, does not falsify the real and turn his science into a study of fictions. The order from quality to quantity to substance is the order of human discovery and induction. For the mathematician does not begin in substance and descend to quantity. Like the philosopher of nature, he gets his notions from the sensible world that incites our senses. He then leaves sensible matter aside.

But once again we are in difficulty. It would look as though in the attempt to rescue geometry from becoming a physics, we are stumbling into the far more serious blunder of exalting mathematics into a metaphysical rank. Would not Aristotle protest that the study of substance belongs to metaphysics and is not the whole scho-

lastic tradition fairly unanimous in the
agreement that substance is properly
analyzed only in the science of being *qua*
being? How can mathematics, whose prov-
ince is usually taken to be the study of
quantity, suddenly turn up with a report
on substance?

Yet scanty reflection will reveal that
mathematics can no more be defined as the
science of quantity than the philosophy of
nature can be termed the science of motion,[38] unless we are speaking in some loose
and unanalyzed sense. In the physical
order, there is the science of mobile being,
and mathematics deals with quantified
being.[39] If this is so, then the mathematician can no more escape from substance
than the philosopher of nature can re-
nounce all interest in the subject of
motion.[40] In tracing the structural hierarchy of substance plus quantity plus
sensible quality in matter, St. Thomas is
concerned to defend the autonomy of
mathematics. A scientific abstraction can

preserve its realism only if it abstracts from a thing those characters which do not depend for being and understanding on what the abstraction leaves out of consideration.[41] In the physical world, for instance, no substantial form can be abstracted from the matter necessary to understand it, and the geometer, for his part, cannot consider accidental form without adverting to the substance on which it depends for existence and definition. In the abstraction of form from matter in geometry, the form concerned is abstracted only from sensible matter. In short, the form abstracted by the mathematical sciences cannot be the form of quantity alone. Since quantity is the measure of substance,[42] and since the measure of a thing is a means of knowing it, geometry must yield some insight into material substance itself, not as sensible but as intelligible.

To deepen this hazy outline of geometrical form in its relation to substance, a distinction must be drawn among the formal, material, and specific parts of any corporeal thing, and the lines dividing them can be best set forth through examples. In the case of man, for instance, the intellect and the will are parts of form, and the various organs of the body are material parts. In the geometrical order, the circumference of a circle is part of its form, and the two semi-circles divided by any diameter are material parts.[43] Now it is obvious that the formal parts of anything physical or mathematical are also parts of its species. But can material parts also be included in the specific parts?

The answer pivots on the relation of whole and part, and on a re-thinking of the realism which enables us to abstract without falsifying. For a whole cannot be abstracted from any parts whatever, since there are some parts on which the whole depends for its being and understanding; man cannot be understood, for instance, without his formal parts. Yet on the other

hand, there are parts on which the whole
does not depend, tonsils for instance in the
case of man; without such parts man can
still be and be understood. Tonsils, hands,
hair, and teeth, though not entering into
the definition of man, the species, are individual material parts. But there are other
material parts without which man cannot
be understood at all. These are the principal material parts, like the heart or the
brain.[44] Such principal material parts, together with the formal parts of any composite, make up the parts of its species.

What has been said in analyzing man
applies also at the mathematical level. A
circle can be understood without its individual parts, like the two semi-circles
into which it could be divided. But *circle*
cannot be defined without reference to an
area. A right angle can be considered
without respect to the two 45° angles into
which it could be bisected; but it cannot
be defined without reference to the extension it includes. Hence, besides the termi-

nating forms in geometry, like the curved line of a circle or the three straight lines of a triangle, there are also principal material parts. Together, the parts of form and the principal parts of matter constitute the species, and it is such a species—triangle, circle, cylinder, ellipsoid, and the like—composed as they are of formal parts and principal material parts, which geometry abstracts as a scientific object.

Yet by what right can such a composite or species still be called a form?

Actually, St. Thomas assigns three different meanings to the word "form" as signifying concretely a reality in the material world. Substantial form is the first act of prime matter, and to study it belongs to the philosophy of nature and to metaphysics. Accidental form is simply a determination of the substantial composite. The accidental form of quantity is where the geometer stops in his abstraction after peeling away the sense qualities of the mobile world, and as terminating

the sensible matter, it has a right to be
called a form and even a mathematical
quality.[45] But this form in the order of
quantity depends on substance to be and
to be understood, and this carries over into
the third meaning of form. For there is
form also in the sense of the composite, the
species, the definition, the essence of a
thing.[46] And it is form in this final meaning, with intelligible matter included, that
any science of mathematics must envision. In brief, the abstraction performed
in geometry relinquishes sensible matter
to regard only substance as subject to
quantity. This, for St. Thomas, is the
meaning of that abstraction of a form, peculiar to the mathematical sciences.

The two-fold meaning of form as the
object of geometry each in its own way,
the one as part and the other as whole,
should be compared for clarification to the
two-fold way of considering *body*. Physically, *body* is a genus, a whole composed
of matter and form and open to further

determination like being alive, being sensate, and being human. Mathematically, on the other hand, *body,* as compared to the physical reality from which it abstracts, is not a whole but a part, referring first to the category of quantity rather than that of substance and defined by its dimensions.[47] To physical, sensible matter, it is related *as* an accident to its subject.[48] That is why St. Thomas can affirm that, with respect to the world of experience, the philosopher of nature abstracts a whole, but that only part of this whole, a part that is as form to sensible matter rather than as accident to substance, is taken into mathematical account.

In its own order, however, and not with respect to the physical world, the mathematical object is not the form of a part *(forma partis)* but a form of a whole *(forma totius)*[49]—an essence, species, definition, quiddity. It is in this sense, where form is taken as a compound of quantity and substance, that mathematics is said to demonstrate through formal causality.[50] Contrary to the direction in the study of nature, where the mind moves largely from effects toward causes and from exterior operations toward knowledge of underlying natures,[51] the geometer proceeds from the definition of a thing to a truly causal knowledge of its properties or effects. Whereas the philosopher of nature starts with the general principles of all mobile being and descends toward species or essences rather late in his career, the mathematician considers specific definitions close to the beginning of his science. All scientific knowledge is causal in structure, and since the species or essence is a form—the form of a whole—the cause considered in mathematical demonstration is the formal cause, embracing a quantitative termination, like a figure, and the matter which it affects.

The formal cause, a principle in mathematical proof, is thus neither substantial form nor accidental form. True enough,

mathematics deals with accidental forms
that bound matter into this or that determinate figure. But no accidental form, abstracted from sensible matter, can be
shaken loose from substance. In the line
of principal material parts, substance falls
within the definitions of geometry, and to
the extent that a measure reveals something of what is measured, mathematics
reports on substance, not in the manner of
what or why it is but how it is extended
and how much. In a similar way, telling
time reports something about time itself
but not its what or why.

Because it does not relinquish intelligible matter, geometry envisions a composite of substance and accident, and its
object, a form of a part with respect to
sensible matter where it exists, is as a form
of a whole in its own order. For if essence
is what makes a thing what it is, then geometrical form requires both quantity and
the substance which underlies it in the real
and completes its definition in our logic.

This composite functions as a form in the sense of terminating the mobile qualities spread out before our senses. Neither substantial nor accidental form alone, the form abstracted in geometry is *sui generis*.

To the mathematician as such, material causality is of no interest. It matters not whether his concept of triangle be abstracted from a church steeple, a pyramid, or a modernistic painting. The stone or iron or pigment, where the triangle exists, does not enter into the definition of a triangle. Similarly, though mathematical realities have efficient causes, it is not under this aspect that they are of interest in geometry,[52] which cares not who build the church or how many men erected the pyramid. Finally, mathematical realities are not studied under the aspect of the good; the geometer does not demonstrate through final causes.[53] A triangle has no appetite to be or to obtain something else in the way of an end. It is simply an essence or form, and it is studied in geometry with the formal cause as the only kind of principle in demonstration.

Having seen now how substance enters into a mathematical object, the picture of quantified being must be sketched more fully by reference to quantity itself. Quantity has two definitions, a formal and a material one. Formally, quantity is defined as an order of parts,[54] and to be more specific, it should be added that the parts are homogeneous, differing among each other only in situs or position.[55] Materially, quantity, or rather quantified being, is "that which is divisible into two or more constituent parts of which each is by nature a 'one' and a 'this.' "[56]

If quantity alone were studied in mathematics, geometry would be part of metaphysics. For like any accident, quantity requires substance to complete its definition, and the mathematician, struggling to study quantity alone, could know it only as the *ens entis* of metaphysics.[57] To make quantified being or quantified substance

the object of mathematical science is
something different. It is to study not
quantity but the quantified. It is to consider an accident defined in the concrete
and therefore requiring substance as the
genus and not the specifying difference in
the definition.[58] In quantified being, there
is a concrete character with quantity
rather than substance as the terminating
or specifying difference, and it is because
of this original character of the quantified,
or of quantity taken in the concrete, that
mathematical sciences form original levels
of knowledge. For a science must predicate an attribute *(passio)* of a subject
through principles.[59] There are at least
four reasons why quantified being yields a
distinctive field for the predication of attributes to subjects and thus opens the
way for a highly distinctive scientific
knowledge which is neither physics nor
logic nor metaphysics.

First of all, quantity inheres in a composite by reason of matter,[60] though its de-

terminate figure is owed to form.[61] Quantity is thus the characteristic accident in a world that has prime matter as a first principle.[62] Because of this affinity with matter, the ultimate substratum in physical things and the primary analogate of receptivity in the whole scale of being, quantity shares in matter's ability to receive.[63] Quantity, as the plurality or multiplicity indicated in its material definition, has a certain openness or indetermination which makes it capable of determination and reception. Indeed, matter, designated by quantity, is the principle of individuation.[64]

In the second place, quantity is the medium by which all other accidents inhere in their material subject,[65] and without quantity all of the qualities and motions of matter would contract to a point. Once more, quantity, as a proximate medium of inherence for other accidents, shows its character in the concrete as a subject.

Thirdly, like any accident, quantity is in the category of predicates; I can say, for instance, "All giraffes are tall," or "The distance to the sun is long." But unlike other accidents, quantity or rather the quantified, admits of being a *per se* subject of a proposition. Thus I can say, "A triangle has three sides," "A straight line is an angle of 180°." Outside of substance, no other material reality taken in the concrete can be a *per se* subject of predication.[66] Again quantity in its concrete setting emerges as something of a subject, with its own proper attributes *(passiones)*. And so the quantified, unlike the other categories of accidents, opens up a whole realm of being to be explored in an original scientific way.

Fourthly, and perhaps most importantly, quantity is the only material reality after substance which admits of division into proper parts.[67] Divisibility, indeed, appears in the material definition of quantity, and hence by its very nature, the quantified has an individuation, distinctness, and independence[68] somewhat like that of substance itself. Because of the substratum in which they are, other accidents receive their individuation; the same shade of green in different blades of grass is different because of the blades. Quantity, however, is divided part by part in its very nature, and hence part by part, it is individuated. Examples can illustrate this notion: A point is defined as a unity having position, and moving it, say from A to B is geometrically impossible. At B, there is simply a different point, and A, the initial point, remains exactly where it was in the co-ordinate system for locating objects. A point, in brief, is individuated by its position, and in another position, the point is simply another individual. Similarly and in terms of position alone, this part of a line is not that. If points and lines are the first principles of quantified being, analogous to matter, form, and privation, the first principles of nature, then quantified being is somehow individuated as a sheer matter of principle.[69]

That is why it is appropriate in geometrical considerations, to speak not only
of genus and difference which are common
to all the categories but of a multiplication
of individuals within species analogous to
the manner of multiplying in the physical
world material substances of the same specific nature.[70] Thus quantity yields not
merely an array of predicates which char-
acterize any science but individuals that
are subjects *par excellence* and make for
the originality of mathematical propositions. Quantity, considered in the abstract,
cannot yield subjects for a scientific analysis; it is a part, like humanity in the case of
man, and predication is only possible in
terms of wholes.[71] Quantified substance,
the object of mathematical sciences, yields
not only attributes but subjects themselves.
The quantified, or simply quantity in the
concrete, can function as both subject and
predicate and thus provide the middle
term in a scientific syllogism.[72] In terms
of quantified being, there can be inde-

pendent mathematical sciences; in terms
of quantity alone, there cannot. Because
of the progressive disregard for substance,
post-Cartesian mathematics has descended
into a study of predicates and tended to
become a logic alone.

The foregoing analysis should sharpen
into focus the role of the imagination in
geometrical knowledge. St. Thomas argues, as we know, that mathematical objects depend upon the imagination and
that the mathematical judgment terminates there, just as judgments in the philosophy of nature terminate in the senses.[73]
But how can this be? How can a domain
of knowledge, dealing only in intelligible
matter, suddenly turn up as accessible to
the imagination? Surely what is intelligible
only cannot simultaneously be imagined,
short of accepting Hume's verdict that
ideas are but faint impressions of a sense
nature.

To answer one question with another,
what is this quantified being that the

mathematical sciences consider? Quantified substance, it was seen, is individuated by its very nature, and the multiplication of parts, for instance, the parts of a straight line, is like the multiplication of physical individuals, for example men within the species *man*. The homogeneous parts of quantified substance are individuated by their situs or position and by that alone. To represent a line or a circle or a triangle, composed as each of them are of homogeneous parts that are individuated, the intellect requires the collaboration of a sense faculty.[74] If there be two straight lines, equal in length and hence members of the same species and individuated only in their respective positions, how can they possibly be kept distinct from each other except in terms of a here and a there, and how can a here and a there be represented without the aid of a power directly representing individuals?

Now the external senses are not equipped to represent geometrical reality since the line or the circle lack color, sound, taste, smell, and texture. Only the internal senses remain, and of the four of them, the only possible candidate to assist the mathematical intellect is the imagination. The cogitative and memorial powers have to do with relations or intentions and not with simple and absolute considerations. And the common or central sense is concerned to organize the data of our external senses and our sensations themselves. But imagination presents objects in the way of simple and absolute consideration. It may truly be said to represent,[75] and it is closely associated with the achievements of the poet.[76] It is perhaps the most speculative of our senses and can be likened to intelligence.[77] And as the activity of the poet would indicate, the imagination in man, just as memory and particularly the cogitative power, is elevated by the presence of a rational soul substantially conjoined to the body.[78] In fact, St. Thomas puts the imagination midway between the external senses, geared as they are toward individuals, and the intellect, the faculty of the universal.[79] More than any of the other senses, human imagination can assist in the making of those products like division and multiplication which makes mathematics a genuine art.[80] A circle or a triangle cannot be perceived by the bodily eye, and yet because of the individuation of their homogeneous parts, a sense power is still needed to represent them. That power is the imagination.

Though charging the imagination with so great a burden, St. Thomas will concede to it only the grasp of individual intelligible matter.[81] To understand pertains quite properly only to the intellect, and to the intellect alone belongs the privilege of grasping the universal intelligible matter which is scientifically analyzed in geometry. The imagination is no more the principal agent of mathematical science than the senses can construct the philosophy of nature. The geometer depends on the imagination to provide phantasms from which he abstracts his universal principles and again to serve as a testing-ground when those principles are resolved to their point of origin in the verification of mathematical judgments. To go beyond parts individuated by their position and hence accessible to the imagination is really to go beyond quantity and to leave the mathematical order behind.

Tooled by the joint efforts of the imagination and the intellect, geometry is a properly human science. God and the angels do not construct mathematical tables and graphs. They do not discourse, moving step by step from one part of a body to another as in measurement and from premises to conclusion as in all of human science. God sees in a single vision all that is stretched out in a divided and multiple manner,[82] in the material world where mathematical realities have their existence though not their definition.

God sees in Himself, as the adequate and simple cause of being, everything that is imitated in a multiple and complex way in His physical effects. But man is closed off from this gaze at the causal side of things. Where God sees the lowest in the highest and the manifold in the one, man must labor in just the opposite direction. Where God sees everything at once, man must limp from one thing to another in a world that is essentially plural and requires the imagination if that plurality is not to be ignored. God is not the Great Mathematician of James Jeans.[83] He simply is. Mathematics, with its diffusion and discursion, can be claimed only by man. In knowing being, the man of wisdom has something in common with all intellects, and mathematics, as a liberal art can do no more than furnish ways to wisdom. In knowing mathematical objects, as opposed to the object of metaphysics, man's knowledge is scattered out like the very quantified being he pursues. In mathematics,

man has run out of intellect that he shares
with a higher world and requires the aid
of the imagination which he shares with
the lower. It is scientific enterprise of a
creature that is on the confines between
the spiritual and material orders, and that
is why it is the easiest, most certain, and
most retainable of human sciences.

So far, the analysis has focused on
quantified being, and the being, or substance, and quantity of mathematical reality have been successively explored.
Geometry, by contrast with arithmetic,
studies continuous quantified being, and
it is time now to turn to a discussion of the
continuum. It is easy to furnish examples
of the continuum—a straight line, an area
enclosed by a circle, the volume of a
sphere. In all such cases, there is a unity,
an uninterrupted extension, a juncture of
parts within a whole.

But when the relation of part to whole
in the continuum is put to closer analysis,
tremendous problems arise. Zeno held that

matter is divided into an infinity of parts
which forbid the apparent motions of nature and turn them into illusions of the
senses. Let us imagine, Zeno argued in
one of his paradoxes, that an arrow is to be
shot by an archer. Forced to traverse an
infinity of points to reach its goal, it can
never on principle reach the target. Moreover, since the very first fraction of the
trajectory contains an infinite multitude of
points, the arrow can never get started at
all.[84] Dormant more or less for centuries
except to be refuted, Zeno has come vigor-
ously back to life in recent geometry and
arithmetic. Ask any Cantorian how many
points there are on a straight line, and he
will answer: An infinity of them![85]

A great impetus to the new infinitism
in mathematics is provided in the so-called
Dedekind cut, where the points on a line
are compared to the members of the number series and where any number, rational
or irrational, can be theoretically defined.

Let us imagine with Dedekind a line

from *A* to *B*, where each point can be put
in correspondence with a real number. To
locate a number like $\sqrt{2}$, let another line
intersect our line *AB* in such a manner that
all of the points corresponding to numbers
less than $\sqrt{2}$ are to the left of the point of
intersection, and all the numbers greater
than $\sqrt{2}$ are to the right. Then $\sqrt{2}$ will be
exactly at the point of intersection. To the
left of the cut, there is no largest number
in the class of numbers, and to the right of
the cut, the class contains no smallest number.[86] Heath finds that "there is an exact
correspondence, almost coincidence between Euclid's definition of equal ratios
and the modern theory of irrationals due
to Dedekind."[87] Whether or not Euclid
thus anticipated Dedekind, the fact remains that the analogy between irrational
numbers and points on a line does suggest
at least a transfinite number of indivisibles
present in a continuum. And Cantor actually drew such a conclusion.

To put the question naively, how many

surfaces are there in the thickness of a
cube? Or how many lines on a surface or
points on a line? A line six inches long, for
instance, can be broken into halves, the
halves into quarters, the quarters into
eighths, and so on. Can a part of the line
finally be attained beyond which division
becomes impossible? Or can the division
simply go on into infinity? Can a solid be
sliced so thin that the third dimension will
finally be cut away and only a surface remain? Or can a line be pulverized into indivisible point-like components? Such, in
different ways, is the problem of the continuum, a problem almost as old as west-
ern philosophy.

And the problem admits of no easy so-
lution. For in the first place, the continuum
itself like quantity may be defined in two
ways, materially and formally, and if one
definition is stressed to the de-emphasis of
the other, an extremism will naturally re-
sult. In its material definition, the continuum is "that which is divisible into

further divisibles";[88] in its formal definition, a continuum is "that whose extremi-
ties are one."[89] Now if there is divisibility
into infinity as required by the first definition, how can there be the unity required
by the second? How can there be parts in
the continuum and hence multiplicity,
while at the same time there is unity and
hence indivisibility?

That a continuum does have parts is
evidenced from our experience of things
physical and from our images of things
mathematical. The right side of a line is
not the left, the apex of a triangle is not
the base, and the rear of a cube is not the
front. There are in fact two kinds of parts
in any continuum. Designated parts, like
the six inches in a six-inch line, measure
their whole,[90] and obviously in dividing
such parts from the whole, division must
eventually cease. In other words, the parts
in our line are finite. Their number is six.
The other and philosophically more inter-
esting kind of parts are the undesignated

parts which are not really distinct from
designated parts but which explain the division of the continuum in a different way.
Such parts, on being divided, form a geometrical series; a line can be divided into
halves, the halves into quarters, and so on
—yielding the series $\frac{1}{2}, \frac{1}{4}, \frac{1}{8}, \frac{1}{16}, \frac{1}{32} \ldots$ [91]
Can this division proceed on to infinity?

Yes and no. The infinity of the continuum consists in this, that no matter how
small a fragment of the whole remains
upon division, there can always be a further fractionation. Nowhere does the division finally terminate in residues that are
indivisible. If the series ended in a point-
like quantity that could no longer be further divided, the original line could never
have been formed; like points, which cannot form lines, lines cannot be added lat-
erally to form planes nor can surfaces,
piled on top of one another ever yield a
third dimension. A point for instance,
could not with its left side touch another
on its right side, so that the two, added

together, would yield a greater extension than the original.[92] Points have no right or left, up or down, front or back. Indivisible, they simply have no parts at all, and touching one another, they would always coincide. Therefore, since the indivisible is never attained by dividing extended quantity, Aristotle could well say that the continuum is always divisible into further divisibles, and from this point of view, the continuum has an infinity of potency for division.

From the viewpoint of act, however, the continuum is always finite in the sense of never being actually divided into an infinity of extended parts. In the division of a line, for instance, it can never be the case that all possible parts are divided from one another. Always the parts that remain upon division are actually finite in number, having only a potency for further division. If a continuum, like a line, were composed of an actual infinity of parts, it would lack all form and determination.[93] For the infinite is the indefinite, the indeterminate, the absolutely plural, open like matter to finitude of form but owning no form and determination of itself.[94] Any definite line has a finite number of parts, a shorter line less and a longer line more.

Thus the continuum is in one sense infinite and in another sense finite. Technically put, the parts of the continuum have a material, privative, or potential infinity in number, so that any one part can always be divided into two more,[95] according to the material definition of the continuum. At any one moment, in accordance with the formal definition of the continuum, the parts of a line are actually finite in number; but what is actually undivided in the order of quantity is potentially divisible and potentially infinite.

Such a conclusion does not mean that the parts exist only potentially in the whole. A line, for instance, has more than merely potential parts; there is an actually existing structure in the line so that one

part is not another and there is an actual
extraposition of parts. When the line receives new parts by way of addition, parts
are added actually to the original. If the
parts of a line existed only in potency, the
intellect could not understand nor could
the imagination represent the lines and
figures of geometry.

If the problem of dividing the continuum refers primarily to the material definition, the question here is rather the unity
or indivision expressed by the formal definition. In some way, the parts of an object like a line have actual existence, and
there are more parts on a long line than
on a short one.[96] Moreover, the parts of a
line are distinguishable even to the point
of being individuated, and if an individual
is that which is undivided in itself and divided from everything else,[97] the individual parts of a continuum must own an actuality as real as that of physical individuals
in a species.

The parts of a continuum, like a line,

can only be individuated if distinguished
by an indivisible boundary between
them.[98] Without such an indivisible divisor
between the parts, the parts themselves
would compenetrate one another; more
than one part would be in the same place;
and parts would no longer be individuated
by their situs. They would in fact melt
into the confusion of the indeterminate.
Yet on the other hand, this boundary cannot be a part like the matter which it
divides. If it were a divisible part and not
an indivisible boundary, it would have a
right and left side, for instance, and the
same problem of rendering the parts distinct and individuated would arise anew.

The part as parts are undivided in
themselves as actually present in the continuum, but they are in potency to further
division. To keep such actually undivided
parts distinct in themselves and distinct
from other parts, the indivisible boundaries between them must likewise be
really and actually present. Such indivisi-

bles terminate each part on the one hand
and on the other continue it with its neigh-
bor.[99]

The same kind of terminative and continuative function is exercised by the *now*
in time. As indivisible, it is not a part of
time, but it terminates the parts in themselves and continues them with each
other.[100] In the permanent mathematical
continuum, the indivisibles likewise iden-
tify parts in themselves and distinguish
them from other parts. They are present
not merely in potency but truly as actual
because the parts themselves are terminated actually, one not being the other,
and continued actually, so that there are
no gaps between them.

What has been said, however, may still
leave not only an obscurity but an apparent contradiction. In reference to the divisibility of the continuum, it was argued
that the parts are present in potency, while
here in dealing with the indivisibles of the
continuum, separating the parts, the em-

phasis is on the parts as present in act. Yet
with the proper distinctions, both conclusions may still be supported. For a line that
did not derive its extension through actual
parts distinct from one another would
have real extension only in potency. To
avoid such mathematical idealism, it must
be conceded that the continuum, prior to
measurement, has actual parts just as a
clover stalk has leaves before we number
them. Numbering adds nothing real to
the leaves; it is only our way of knowing
their quantity, for in no other manner
could we know how many leaves there are.
In a similar way, measurement does not
endow the parts of a continuum with their
objective determination but merely reveals
how many parts there are. As in the count-
ing of the clover leaves, measure numbers
the actually existing continuous parts.[101]

Something similar goes on in the telling of time. The *now* of time is one in
reality but divided by human logic into
two *now's*, the one terminating the past

and the other opening the future.[102] In numbering the successive parts of the temporal continuum, the mind considers the single indivisible to be first the term of one part and secondly the principle of the part immediately following. In both the temporal and the mathematical continuum, parts have a real priority and posteriority. Far from being compenetrated and confused, they are outside of one another and distinct. The number of actual parts in quantity is always finite, but by division this number can be made larger and larger *ad infinitum.*

If the number of actual parts in any continuum is actually finite, then there must be minimal parts in act, divisible and distinguishable only in potency. And the question arises: How big are these minimal parts? How long is the minimal part actually existing on a line, for instance? Such questions are not answerable in geometry since they cannot be solved in terms of measurement. For the minimal

actual parts of a continuum cannot by
themselves have any size except virtually
or potentially. Principles of measurement,
they cannot be measured themselves, just
as unity is a principle of number but, not
being plural, cannot be a number itself. As
unity is a minimal quantity in arithmetic,
so measure takes place in terms of a mini-
mum which is a principle of measurement,[103] but not the thing measured.

Minimal parts, actually existing, are of
course potentially divisible into a new genus of parts. But when this potency is reduced to act, the minimal parts of the new
wholes enjoy, in their new independence,
only a virtual size. As principles of measure within their new genus, they are not
measured within the genus itself. The
problem of the size of a minimal part is
thus not solved by dividing the part; it is
only shifted and re-stated. In short, the
principles of any science are not proved
by the science employing them. Principles
are only inadequately and virtually the

wholes which they principiate; otherwise, in knowing the principles, the mind would also actually know what is principiated.[104] Unlike multitude, unity is not numbered; unlike the whole continuum, a minimal part is not reduced to measure. To know and to show that there are minimal parts in a mathematical continuum is the task of metaphysics, examining the principles of mathematics. And metaphysics reports on the minimal part not by measuring it, as geometry would proceed, but by showing that it *is* in accordance with the formal object of metaphysics itself.

To separate the parts of a line that already are distinct one from the other is to convert the indivisible which, prior to separation, is both terminative and continuative into what is terminative only. But if this actual dividing or separating of parts does not take place precisely at the limit-like indivisible but within the parts themselves, then the new parts, present only potentially before the actual division, are reduced to actual presence.[105]

To summarize this brief analysis of the continuum, there are parts actually existing in any extended quantity, making it to be determinate and distinct. Such parts are actually finite in number but potentially infinite through division. The minimal parts must not be confused with the indivisible boundaries between them. For the minimal parts are divisible. Their boundaries are not.

In terms of these indivisible limits between the parts of the continuum, new light can be shed on geometry in its relationship to the real world. Because of the indivisibles, the circle, for instance, even with its precisely mathematical circumference and center, does exist in the sensible world, but it is not thought of in geometry as having this existence.[106] The triangle, the line, even the point have a similar existence in the world of experience, and even in the case of a polygon

with 10,000 sides, it can be said that because of the way in which lines exist in
sensible matter the polygon actually exists
on the surface of the desk top before me.
But it is not studied as having this existence.

Mathematics, in short, deals with
things that depend on matter for their existence but not for their definition and are
known by abstraction which leaves sensible qualities aside. As there are indivisible points on a line, so there are indivisible
lines in a plane, and indivisible planes in a
solid. It is true that in their real character,
indivisibles like the points on a line or the
lines in a plane exist in a simultaneously
terminating and continuing function.
However, in mathematical abstraction, the
mind considers their terminating role
alone, in order to bring this or that figure
into scientific focus. Such a termination of
matter is accidental form,[107] and this the
geometer abstracts. But the form in ques-

tion cannot be abstracted from intelligible matter.

If substance, quantity, and the terminations of quantity are real, geometrical abstraction does not warp its object, but only makes distinctions within the real to liberate, so to speak, the figures and lines it will study.[108] Leaving aside sense quality and motion, geometry is not a physics, but neither is it a logical idealization through constructs. Truth in geometry, like truth in all science, is not an affair of consistency but of conformity between mind and reality. Geometry is concerned with the real, imaginable, and formal but not with the physical, sensible, or logical. It studies essence or species but not natures which add mobility to essence[109] and refer to final causes. Concerned with the real and having a real basis, geometry uses imagination not because it is free to construct any chimerical figure in the name of science but primarily because in going beyond the imagination it would go beyond quantity itself.

St. Thomas identifies the continuum with intelligible matter,[110] and in this perspective, the object of geometry can now be better understood. The geometer studies a matter-form composite, an essence or species. He may demonstrate through the indivisible boundaries of a continuum, the points, lines, and planes that are as forms respectively to the lines, planes, and solids which they terminate; he may also prove through matter, as in showing that the angle inscribed in a semi-circle is a right angle.[111] Such demonstrations, apparently in terms of material causes, are actually in terms of intelligible matter,[112] and hence they are still within the focus of the formal cause, where form is considered the form of a whole. The indivisibles, terminating the continuum as a whole or terminating each actually existing part and continuing it with its neighbors, are as forms; what is terminated is as matter.

What is indivisible in the continuum is emphasized by the formal definition; what is divisible but actually terminated, by the material definition. The parts of quantity, so terminated, pertain to intelligible matter, to substance as subject to quantity.

Just as substance claims quantity before sensible quality, so prior to terminating figure within the genus of quantity itself material substance is quantified by indeterminate dimensions rendering the parts distinguishable. The substance is actual, and so are the unterminated dimensions, and the composite of the two, which is something divisible, may be properly termed intelligible matter. Under this aspect, quantity is taken as dividing but not as terminating, and together with the matter-form composite which is substance unterminated quantity confers the form of corporeity.[113]

Subjected to indeterminate dimensions, substance is intelligible matter. It is a continuum in its material sense, open to the further function of quantity as terminating its parts into this or that figure or line which is quantity in its formal sense. Taken alone, substance has no parts except matter and form that are its causes; with indeterminate dimensions, it has actual quantitative parts that belong to intelligible matter. Such a compound of substance and indeterminate quantity is as matter in the object of geometry; circles and triangles are as forms. The composite is a form of a whole, and hence the dualism of divisible matter and terminating form is best exemplified by the continuum.

Geometry is hence not a study of an ideal order but a science of the real world —how else could it be called a science? It is not of course confined to the actual any more than metaphysics is prohibited from a study of possible being. Although there is no motion, not even potency, in mathematical objects, there is in geometry a distinction of actuality and possibility, just as in metaphysics itself. Beginning with a line of finite length, for instance, one may extend it as far as he wishes into the realm of possibility—by what Aristotle regarded as the mathematical infinity of a line, that to which something can always be added. But this protraction no more robs geometry of its right as a science of the real than metaphysics is de-realized when extended to consider possible being. The intelligible matter of geometry, the substance with unterminated dimensions of quantity, is truly real, so are the terminating indivisible forms, so indeed is the object of geometry, the form abstracted from sensible matter under the name of continuous quantified substance. And the mathematical abstraction, considering the indivisible terminations and the unterminated matter to which they apply, considers objects that exist in the sensible world although not thought of mathematically as bearing this existence.

In mathematics, where what is better known to us and in itself coincide, arith-

metic, known prior to geometry, is in itself
more knowable.[114] As a lower science is to
a higher like matter to form rather than
species to genus,[115] so number in the formal order is prior to the continuum, but
materially the continuum is prior to number.[116] The continuum provides the material to be enumerated, while number is
the measure of such material.[117] The continuum is, as it were, a matrix whose division yields number and whose divisibility
into a potential infinity of parts affords a
real basis for the principle that number is
also potentially infinite.[118] What is first
known to the native intellect is being, then
division or discrete quantity, then unity
which is a measure, and finally multiplicity
which the unity reduces to number.[119] Such
is the order in which reality is known to
the natural intellect, beginning its career
not with being and unity as studied meta-
physically but with their counterparts in
the sensible world. The primitive idea of
division derives from discrete quantity,

that of unity from a negation of this division; and finally the multiplicity, measured by unity into number, is likewise of a quantitative order.[120] Because the continuum is materially or ontologically prior to number which measures it, it is more material in the sense of substantial than number which is more intelligible in the sense of a terminating form, and so the continuum is the typical case of how substance enters into mathematical consideration.

The object of geometry is continuous, quantified substance, a form of a whole in its own order. Intelligible matter or substance with unterminated quantity is as matter in this form of a whole and accidental terminations are as forms of the part. This form of a whole is an essence, a formal cause, the species in the mathematical order and, a totality in its own right, is a form of the part with respect to the physical whole from which the mathematician makes a truly formal abstraction. So at least one can telescope the object of geometry from the texts of St. Thomas. But Thomas Aquinas would be the first to protest if the discussion ended in his texts and if the telescope did not scan the rival systems to absorb their truth and avoid their error. Although a full-dress treatment of modern geometry is excluded here by the practical limits of a lecture, it is useful to glance briefly at the typical problems created by non-Euclidian geometries to see what a Thomist might contribute to the debate. The formalist approach to mathematics would allow as many different geometries as the sets of freely chosen postulates which are consistent, complete, and mutually independent. The generalized theory of relativity, holding that a geometry can be tested by physical experiment, has decided upon the non-Euclidian character of our universe.

Almost as though writing a casebook for what Aristotle said in the *Posterior Analytics*, Euclid begins his famous work, *The Elements*, with twenty-three defini-

tions of basic geometrical entities; five
postulates, required specifically for his
science; and five common notions, pre-
supposed to any scientific thinking what-
soever.[121] Among these prolegomena to
Euclid's demonstrations is the famous fifth
postulate on parallelism: "That, if a
straight line falling on two straight lines
make the interior angles on the same side
less than two right angles, the two straight
lines, if produced indefinitely, meet on
that side on which are the angles less than
the two right angles."[122] As it is often put
in equivalent form and in a manner that
makes it easier to confront rival notions,
the parallel postulate says that through a
given point not on a given line one and
only one parallel can be drawn in a given
plane. In the so-called hyperbolic geometry, developed by Bolyai and Lobat-
schevsky, not only one but many non-in-
tersecting lines can be drawn with respect
to a given line in a given plane through the
same given point; and in the elliptical ge-

ometry proposed by Riemann, no line parallel to a given line can be drawn through
a given point on a plane.

From antiquity in the works of Proclus
and Ptolemy down to modern times in the
writings of Saccheri, Lambert, and Legen-
dre, various attempts have been made to
prove the fifth postulate of Euclid.[123] All
such ambitions have failed to demonstrate
what Euclid took as a postulate and therefore as indemonstrable in mathematics.
Where they appeared to triumph, it was
only because somewhere in their proofs
they had assumed what they needed to
prove. For instance, if you assume two
lines in the same plane as equidistant and
then go on to give a geometrical "proof"
of their parallelism, you are only begging
the question by taking an equivalent to
the postulate as a starting-point. Something of the same sort of assumption must
have been made in Aristotle's time, for he
reports that the then current theories of
parallelism beg the question.[124] Euclid's

achievement appears to have been to take the proposition about parallels for what it actually is, a postulate that geometry cannot demonstrate.[125]

With different postulates, modern geometry has constructed two alternatives to Euclid.

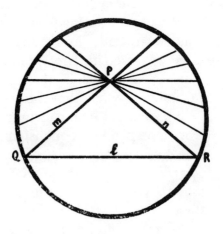

Fig 1

In hyperbolic geometry, it is postulated that given a line l and a point P not on this line, there are at least two lines through P which do not intersect l. Such lines may be illustrated by considering the interior of a conic section like a circle (figure 1). Consider now the two lines m and n, drawn through P in such a manner that in a Euclidian problem they would intersect the circumference at points Q and R on line l. But since the only points in the hyperbolic plane are on the interior of the circle, Q and R do not exist, and hence m and n do not intersect l in the plane under consideration. Through the cross angles formed by m and n, a whole bundle of lines can be drawn which, in the hyperbolic plane, do not intersect l.[126]

In the elliptical case, there is still another alternative to Euclid's fifth postulate. This time, a straight line is assumed as an arrangement that returns to its point of origin and encloses a space.[127] The easiest approach to this kind of geometry is through considering the surface of a sphere. Great circles on this surface always intersect one another, and it is not possible, in spherical, or more generally elliptical, geometry to draw parallels in Euclid's sense.

For each of these non-Euclidian systems, there are special theorems, such as the proposition in connection with a triangle that the sum of the interior angles is less than 180° in hyperbolic geometry and more than 180° in the elliptical case. Proof has been given by Cayley and Klein that the two non-Euclidian systems are self-consistent.[128] Both can be constructed through suitable transformations of projective geometry.[129] Both are useful in different practical ways, and both are good exercises for the mind which is one of the functions of mathematics as a liberal art.

But the question arises to the comparative scientific value of Euclid and his modern rivals.[130] Is the priority of one geometry over another still an open and perhaps insoluble question, so that the mind may take its pick among the three different postulates about parallelism and freely construct a geometry without challenge to the postulates themselves? Is one of the geometries just as good, just as scientific, just as geometrical as the other except that this or that system may happen to have better practical applications in a given field of problems or require fewer and simpler postulates?

Einstein holds that the space immediately around us is approximately Euclidian but that over vast stretches of the universe the parallel postulate of Euclid must yield to the elliptical geometry of Riemann. But by its nature as a system of physics, relativity mechanics would test a geometry in the mobile world of sensible matter, whereas mathematics prescinds from all motion and sense qualities. Einstein would convert space from a mathematical entity, synonymous with the extension of bodies,[131] into a physical and natural re-

ality like place and time where the mobile
is added to the quantified. Geometry is
thus applied beyond geometry without regard to the hierarchy which puts physics
and mathematics into two different formal
orders of scientific knowledge.

Quantified but not mobile, space is an
order of homogenous parts, differentiated
only by their position and not by any physical heterogeneities as in the relativistic
fields. In the fourth postulate of *The Elements*,—"that all right angles are equal to
one another,"—[132] Euclid was paying
mathematical respect to the proposition,
examined in metaphysics, that quantity
does not involve the variability and change
that charges throughout the natural, physical universe. In its species, a triangle
here is the same as a triangle there, and it
is the same in the twentieth century as it
was in the nineteenth. Unlike place with
which it is often confused, space is uniform, because it is only the extended quantity of a body or of the universe of bodies.

Structurally, such extended quantity is prior to sensible quality, in accordance with a preceding analysis, and the mind considers the first to be a receptacle for the second. This equates space and continuous quantity. Taken alone, space, like the quantified, does not embrace in definition the mobile qualities of the physical order which Einstein uses as a test of a geometry.

From a more positive angle, if the quantified is truly homogeneous as metaphysics can show and as Euclid affirms in his fourth postulate, then the lines that are parallel in so-called ordinary space approximating the dimensions of the human body will continue to remain parallel no matter how far the lines are extended where the quantified is considered without the sensible qualities superadded. The sameness, uniformity, homogeneity in the quantified order itself will insure that the distance obtaining between the lines, no matter what their length, remains the same. Differences in position as the lines are extended only add new parts, each individuated by their situs and unchanged in their specific character in being, for instance the parts of a straight line.

Putting his proposition about parallels among the postulates rather than theorems, Euclid was unerringly right. Postulates are assumptions made by a science unequipped to establish them. But is an assumption in geometry therefore an assumption absolutely? If our physics cannot check our geometry, is there no other way of testing our postulates except by such purely logical norms as consistency and completeness?

To solve this question, there is an old Aristotelian maxim that no science can examine its own principles because the principles must be employed by the science to make any of its specific demonstrations. Yet while unable to demonstrate the principles of his discipline, a scientist has two important escapes from utter relativism. First of all, he can reach his principles by

dialectics,[133] and secondly, he can submit
them for critical analysis to that ruling
science of human sciences which is metaphysics.[134] He should not, as in relativity,
submit his principles to a lower science,
like physics. Aristotle provides striking examples of dialectical reasoning in the first
book of the Physics and in the fourth book
of the Metaphysics, and he has studied the
process analytically in the Topics. Much
of the Metaphysics is an analysis of the
basic concepts found in other sciences, like
quantity, motion, the whole and the part,
the four causes, the infinite.

To summarize this appraisal of elliptical geometry, the parallel postulate of Euclid is not capable of geometrical demonstration, but this does not free it into the
realm of arbitrary assumption. Granted
that on the level of demonstration, the
three geometries now existing cannot challenge one another, it is still possible to decide on their merits in a dialectical debate.
Does quantity include motion? Is quantity

homogeneous? Can the multiplication of individual parts change their species? Such questions can be dialectically raised and answered by the geometer, and it is further necessary to allow postulates dialectically known in mathematics to be scientifically examined in metaphysics, the science of sciences.

The hyperbolic case is complicated but still within the reach of dialectics as a means of reaching principles and of metaphysics as a means of their defense. If St. Thomas is right in his analysis of the continuum, there is no "cut" between the points on the interior of a circle and the points on the circumference. The circle is a continuum of homogeneous parts, and the points on the periphery are not partlike structures between the inside and the outside of the figure but indivisibles at the limits of both, terminating the interior and exterior regions each in itself and continuing them with one another. If St. Thomas is right, there is no such cleavage between the interior and circumference of the circle as the hyperbolic plane required in the example chosen. This is not a demonstrative argument; it is only dialectical. But dialectics is a way for the mathematician to decide his premises when, reaching back to the principles of his science, he runs out of demonstration in his own order.

All such arguments as these should not imply that non-Euclidian geometries are wrong or to be scrapped in favor of a monopoly by the Euclidian system. As dialectics, they are worthwhile constructions, and they have of course important measuring applications in the physical order as relativity theory attests. But the problem is whether or not the non-Euclidian systems give a scientific knowledge of continuous quantified being which exists in sensible matter but is not regarded by the geometer as having this existence. If St. Thomas was right as a philosopher of the quantified, then Euclid enjoys priority as

the geometer of the real world. He was
philosopher enough to know what he was
doing. He knew that to have a science he
needed principles or postulates that his
own science could not examine. He therefore stated his principles and divided them
in logical form. Euclid's fourth and fifth
postulates concern the uniformity of quantity. They are propositions couched in
terms of mathematical signs, or mathematical effects, of a principle examined in
metaphysics that the quantified is homogeneous and space isotropic. Whatever
the great positive value of modern geometries may be, Euclid's system is the science
of the continuous, quantified substance
that exists in reality, a science that owns
premises true, primary, immediate, better
known than, prior to, and causal of their
conclusions.[135]

Finally, and perhaps most importantly, the metaphysical analysis of mathematics reveals that the points and lines and
figures of geometry are defined in intel-

ligible matter. Such matter, to repeat, is
substance invested with quantity that is
unterminated in its dimensions. This is by
no means the matter of non-Euclidian geometries. Indeed, the matter in which the
non-Euclidian lines are drawn is terminated, as hyperbolical in one case and elliptical in another. Hence, the non-Euclidian systems do not compete with Euclid
because they are not talking about the
same thing. The non-Euclidian systems
go beyond quantity. Their matter is not
homogeneous parts but heterogeneity and
curvature. It is no longer intelligible matter but sensible matter, terminated into
this or that form or figure in the fourth
species of quality. That is why non-Euclidian systems lend themselves to physical
interpretation.

Intelligible matter is something different. It says only substance endowed with
unterminated homogenous parts individuated by their position. Different positions
involve only different individuals of the

same species of part. They do not change
the species from, say, a straight line in one
portion of space to a curving line in another. If unterminated quantity is not the
same as terminated quantity, if quantity
differs from quality, if quantified being involves only substance with homogeneous
parts open to further determination
through form and figure, if quantified being has from within itself no principles of
motion or change, then Euclid remains the
geometer of the truly geometrical world.
Twenty-five hundred years have no more
changed the basic truths of his system than
they have changed the basic insights of
Aristotle. He organized a body of scientific knowledge that stands distinct from
all others and is not testable in the physical
sensible matter where a geometry like Riemann's has scored its great triumphs.

Euclidian geometry is the science of
what is real but not physical, imaginable
but not sensible, truly essential but not
natural and mobile. Dependent on meta-

physics, it is not metaphysics. With its object that exists in the physical world, it is nevertheless not a physics. Abstracting form from matter, it is not formal in the second-intentional and logical sense. A science in its own right with a distinctive and original set of principles and an object that exists in the real world, Euclid's system is neither a physics nor a logic nor a metaphysics. It is, after all, geometry.

NOTES

The edition of each work cited in these notes is given in the first citation; thereafter, citations to that work refer to that edition.

1. The object of geometry is being understood here as the answer to the question: What does the mind envision as the speculable reality which specifies the habit of geometry? *In Boet. de Trin.*, ed. Wyser, V, 1, c. In other words, I intend to leave aside the broad problem about the object of science in general, its material and formal parts, and the distinction, whatever it be, between the formal object *quo* and the formal object *quod,* in scientific knowledge. Such precise differentiations, which constitute a study by themselves, are not necessary to the understanding of the following analysis. It is equally unnecessary here to labor a distinction between the object and subject of a science. On the formal objects *quo* and *quod* and on the subject of a science, cf. *In I Anal. Post.*, ed. Leon., 41, nn. 6-13.

2. Cf., for instance, *The Meaning of Relativity,* 3rd ed. (Princeton, 1950), pp. 4, 64; H. Robertson's essay, "Geometry as a Branch of Physics," in *Albert Einstein: Philosopher-Scientist,* ed. P. Schilpp (Evanston, Ill., 1949) pp. 315-332.

3. Cf., for instance B. Russell, *The Principles of Mathematics,* 2nd ed. (New York, 1948), pp. 3-9.

4. *In III Met.,* ed. Cathala, 2, n. 349.

5. *In XI Met.,* 4, n. 2208.

6. *In I Phy.,* 1, n. 8; *In I Met.,* 2, n. 46.

7. *In Boet. de Trin.,* VI, 3, c.; *In I Anal. Post.,* 4, n. 15.

8. *In I Anal. Post.,* 4, n. 16.

9. *In lib. de Causis,* ed. Vives, 1; *In VI Eth.,* ed. Pirotta, 7, nn. 1208-1210; *In Boet. de Trin.,* V, 1, ad 3.

10. *In Boet. de Trin.,* VI, 1, *ad sec. quest., c.*

11. *In de Mem. et Rem.,* ed. Vives, 5.

12. *In Boet. de Trin.,* V, 1, *ad primam quest., c.*

13. *Summa Theol.,* I, q. 84, a. 7, c; cf. also,

ibid., I, q. 85, a. 8, c; *In III de Anima,* ed. Pirotta, 8, n. 717.

14. *In VI Eth.*, 1, n. 1121.

15. *In V Met.*, 13, n. 949; *Summa Theol.*, I, q. 11, a. 2, ad 4, and I, q. 78, a. 3, ad 2; *In Boet. de Trin.*, V, 1, ad 10; Aristotle, *Topics*, VI, 4, 141b 5-15.

16. *In I Phys.*, 1, nn. 6-11; *In I Met.*, 2, n. 46; *In Boet. de Trin.*, V, 2, c.

17. *In I Phys.*, 1, n. 2.

18. *Summa Theol.*, I, q. 85, a. 1, ad 2; *In I de Anima*, 2, n. 28.

19. *In Boet. de Trin.*, V, 3, c (*circa fin.*)

20. *Ibid.*, also, *Summa Theol.*, I, q. 40, a. 3, c; *Comp. Theol.*, ed. Vives, 62.

21. *Summa Theol.*, I, q. 85, a. 1, c; *In III de Anima*, 1, n. 577.

22. *In I Anal. Post.*, 30, n. 5.

23. Cf. St. Thomas' notion of *separatio* in *In Boet. de Trin.*, V, 3, c.

24. *Summa Theol.*, I, q. 85, a. 1, ad 2.

25. *In Boet. de Trin.*, V, 3, c.

26. *Ibid.; Summa Theol.*, I, q. 40, a. 3, c.

27. *Summa Theol.*, I, q. 85, a. 1, ad 2; *In VIII Met.*, 5, n. 1760; *In I de Anima*, 2, n. 28; *In III de Anima*, 8, nn. 710, 714.

28. *In II Met.*, 10, n. 2339; *In IV Phys.*, 1, n. 7.

29. *Summa contra Gent.*, ed. Vives, I, 82.

30. *Summa Theol.*, I, q. 82, a. 1, ad 2.

31. *In Boet. de Trin.*, V, 3, c; *In II Phys.*, 3, n. 5; *In III de Anima*, 8, n. 707; *Summa Theol.*, I, q. 85, a. 1, c. and ad 2.

32. *In I Phys.*, 12, n. 10.

33. *In II Phys.*, 3, n. 5; *In I de Coelo, ed. Leon.*, 1, n. 2.

34. *In II Phys.*, 5, n. 11; *In II Sent.*, ed. Vives, d. 9, q. 1, a. 1, 1; *In II Anal. Post.*, 8, n. 3.

35. *Summa contra Gent.*, I, 44.

36. *In I Anal. Post.*, 16, n. 5.

37. *In VII Phys.*, 5, n. 5.

38. John of St. Thomas, *Curs. Phil. I. Phil. Nat.*, ed. Reiser, I. P, q. i, a. i, pp. 7 ff.

39. *In IV Met.*, 1, n. 532.

40. For St. Thomas, the subject of motion is known to the philosopher of nature by induction. *In I Phys.*, 12, n. 10.

41. *In Boet. de Trin.*, V, 3, c.

42. *In I Eth.*, 7, n. 95; *In IX Met.*, 1, n. 1768; *In Boet. de Trin.*, IV, 2, c.

43. *In VII Met.*, 9, n. 1475; *Ibid.*, 10, n. 1483; *In I Anal. Post.*, 10, n. 3.

44. *In Boet. de Trin.*, V, 3, c.; *In VII Met.*, 10, n. 1489; *In II Phys.*, 5, n. 4.

45. *In Boet. de Trin.*, V, 3, c. (*circa fin.*)

46. *Summa Theol.*, I, q. 85, a. 4, ad 4; *In V Met.*, 2, n. 764; *In II Phys.*, 11, nn. 4, 8.

47. *In Boet. de Trin.*, V, 3, ad 2; *In X Met.*, 2, n. 1952; *Summa Theol.*, I, q. 7, a. 3, c; *De Ente et Ess.*, trans. A. Maurer (Toronto, 1949) c. 2.

48. *Summa Theol.*, I, q. 3, a. 7, c; *In III Met.*, 13, n. 514.

49. *In VII Met.*, 9, nn. 1467-1469.

50. "In scientiis enim mathematicis proceditur per ea tantum, quae sunt de essentia rei, cum demonstrent solum per causam formalem;

et ideo non demonstratur in eis aliquid de una re per aliam rem, sed per propriam definitionem illius rei." *In Boet. de Trin., ed. cit.,* VI, 1, c. (*ad primam questionem.*) Cf. also, *In I Anal. Post.,* 4, n. 16; *In I Phys.,* 1, n. 5.

51. *In Boet. de Trin.,* VI, 1, c. (*ad primam questionem*).

52. *Summa Theol.,* I, q. 44, a. 1, ad 3.

53. *Ibid.,* I, q. 5, a. 4, ad 4; *In III Met.,* 4, n. 375.

54. *De Ver.,* ed. Spiazzi, II, 9, c; *Summa Theol.,* I, q. 14, a. 12, ad 1; *ibid.,* I, q. 12, a. 12, ad 1.

55. *In Boet. de Trin.,* V, 3, ad 3; *Summa Theol.,* III, q. 77, a. 2, c.

56. This is Aristotle's definition of *quantum.* Met., V, 13, 1020a 7-9. Cf. *The Basic Works of Aristotle,* ed. R. McKeon (New York, 1941) p. 766. For St. Thomas briefer definition, cf. *In V Met.,* 15, n. 977.

57. *Summa Theol.,* I, q. 45, a. 4, c.

58. *De Ver.,* III, 7, ad 2; *De Ente et Ess.,* c. 4; *Summa Theol.,* I-II, q. 53, a. 2, ad 3.

59. *In I Anal. Post.*, 10, n. 8.

60. *In V Met.*, 9, n. 892.

61. *In II de Anima*, 8, n. 332.

62. St. Thomas agrees with Aristotle that "materia sit maxime substantia." *In VII Met.*, 2, n. 1278.

63. *Summa Theol.*, I, q. 76, a. 6, ad 2; *Qu. Dis. de Anima*, ed. Vives, 7.

64. *In Boet de Trin.*, ed. Vives, IV, 2, ad 3; *In V Met.*, 8, n. 876; *De Ente et Ess.*, c. 2.

65. *In I Phys.*, 3, n. 4; *In III de Anima*, 8, n. 707.

66. *In V Met.*, 15, n. 983; *In I Anal. Post.*, 2, n. 5.

67. *In Boet. de Trin.*, ed. Vives, IV, 2, ad 3; *In V Met.*, 2, n. 5.

68. Hence quantity is first said of the discrete and secondarily of the continuous. *De Ver.*, II, 10, c.; *Summa contra Gent.*, I, 69; *In V Eth.*, 5, n. 939.

69. "No accident, however, has in itself the proper nature of division, unless it is quan-

tity; therefore, dimensions of themselves have a certain nature of individuation according to a determined place, inasmuch as place is a difference of quantity." *In Boet. de Trin.*, IV, 2, ad 3. English translation from *The Trinity and the Unicity of the Intellect*, tr. Sr. Rose Emmanuella Brennan (St. Louis, 1946) pp. 111-112; cf. also, *ibid.*, ed Wyser, V, 3, ad 3.

70. *In III de Anima*, 8, nn. 709-716.

71. *De Ente et Ess.*, c. 2.

72. John of St. Thomas, *Curs. Phil. I Ars Log.*, II P., q. viii, pp. 405 ff.

73. *In Boet. de Trin.*, VI, 2, c.

74. *In VII Met.*, 10, n. 1494.

75. "Dicuntur autem intelligibilia, hujusmodi singularia, secundum quod absque sensu comprehenduntur per solam phantasiam, quae quandoque intellectus vocatur secundum illud in tertio de Anima: 'Intellectus passivus corruptibilis est.'" *Ibid.*

76. *In I Anal. Post.*, 1, n. 6.

77. *De Pot.*, ed. Pession, II, 6, ad 2; *In VIII Met.*, 10, n. 1494; *In IX Eth.*, 7, n. 1214.

78. *De Pot.*, II, 2, c.

79. *Summa Theol.*, I, q. 55, a. 2, ad 2.

80. *In Boet. de Trin.*, V, 1, ad 3; *Summa Theol.*, I, q. 57, a. 3, ad 3.

81. *In III de Anima*, 8, n. 715; *In VIII Met.*, 10, n. 1495.

82. *Summa Theol.*, I, q. 12, a. 12, ad 1; I, q. 57, a. 2, c; *Summa contra Gent.*, I, 51.

83. *The Mysterious Universe* (New York, 1937), pp. 165, 168.

84. Aristotle, *Phys.*, VI, 2, 233a 21 ff, *The Basic Works of Aristotle, op. cit.*, pp. 320-321.

85. An authoritative treatment of this subject will be found in K. Godel, *The Consistency of the Axiom of Choice and of the Generalized Continuum-Hypothesis with the Axioms of Set Theory* (Princeton, 1940), *passim.*

86. R. Dedekind, *Essays on the Theory of Numbers* (Chicago, 1901), pp. 11-21.

87. T. Heath, *The Thirteen Books of Euclid's Elements* (Cambridge, 1908), II, 124.

88. *In VI Phys.*, 1, n. 6; *In III Phys.*, 1, n. 3.

89. *In III Phys.*, 1, n. 3; *In VI Phys.*, 1, n. 2.

90. *In V Met.*, 21, n. 1093.

91. *In I Phys.*, 9, n. 12.

92. *In VI Phys.*, 1, nn. 4-5.

93. *In III Phys.*, 12, n. 2.

94. *Ibid., In III Phys.*, 11, n. 6.

95. *Summa Theol.*, I, q. 7 (*tota questio*).

96. *Summa contra Gent.*, II, 49; *In de Sensu et Sensato*, ed. Vives, 15.

97. *In Boet. de Trin.*, ed. Vives, II, 2, ad 3.

98. *In VI Phys.*, 1, n. 7; *ibid.*, 5, n. 6; *Summa Theol.*, I, q. 8, a. 2, ad 2.

99. *In III de Anima*, 3, n. 609.

100. *In IV Phys.*, 18, n. 10.

101. *In V Met.*, 8, nn. 872-875.

102. *In IV Phys.*, 18, n. 5; *De Pot.*, IV, 2, ad 13.

103. *In X Met.*, 2, nn. 1945-1946.

104. E. g., ". . . omnes proprietates numerum in unitate *quodammodo* praeexistunt." *De Ver.*, II, 1, c.

105. J. of St. Thomas, *Curs. Phil. I. Phil. Nat.*
      I P., q. xx, a. 1, p. 421.

106. *In I Phys.*, 1, n. 2.

107. *Summa Theol.*, I, q. 7, a. 1, ad 2; *Ibid.*,
      I, q. 7, a. 3, c.

108. *In II Phys.*, 3, n. 5; *In XI Met.*, 1, n. 2162.

109. *De Ente et Ess.*, c. 2.

110. *De Ver.*, ed. cit., II, 6, c; *In I Anal. Post.*,
      41, n. 5; *In VII Met.*, 10, n. 1496, 11, n. 1508;
      In VIII Met., 5, nn. 1760-1761.

111. *In II Anal. Post.*, 9, n. 6.

112. *In Boet. de Trin.*, V, 3, ad 4.

113. *In VII Met.*, 10, nn. 1496-1499; *In I Anal.*
      Post., 4, n. 5; *In VIII Met.*, ed. cit., 5, nn.
      1760-1761. Prior to terminating figure, sub-
      stance possesses matter with undetermined
      dimensions. (*In Boet. de Trin.*, ed. Vives,
      IV, 2, c). Such dimensions are quantity *ut
      dividente* and not *ut terminante* and make
      substance to be *materia intelligibilis . . .
      secundum quod aliquid divisibile accipitur.*
      In I Anal. Post., 4, n. 5. J. of St. Thomas,
      Curs. Theol., ed. Vives, I, q. 6, d. 6, a. 2,
      no. xx.

114. *In X Met.*, 2, nn. 1939-1943.

115. Cajetan, *In De Ente et Ess.*, ed. Laurent, (proemium), p. 7.

116. *In Boet. de Trin.*, ed. Vives, IV, 2, ad 6.

117. *In III Phys.*, 12, nn. 3-6; *In III de Anima*, 1, n. 578.

118. *In V. Phys.*, 5, n. 9.

119. *Summa Theol.*, I, q. 11, a. 2, ad 4.

120. *Ibid.*, I, q. 85, a. 8, c. It would appear here that St. Thomas is dealing with the natural, pre-scientific intellection of man as conditioned by mathematical division and indivision.

121. Heath, *op. cit.*, I, 153-155.

122. *Ibid.*, p. 155.

123. *Ibid.*, pp. 204-219.

124. *Prior Anal.*, II, 16, 65a 4, *The Basic Works of Aristotle, op. cit.*, p. 94.

125. Euclidian postulates seem to conform to Aristotle's "thesis": "I call an immediate basic truth of syllogism a 'thesis' when, though it is not susceptible of proof by the

teacher, yet ignorance of it does not constitute a total bar to progress on the part of
the pupil. . . ." *Post Anal.*, I, 72a 15-17,
The Basic Works, op. cit., pp. 112-113.

126. Cf. H. DeBaggis, "Hyperbolic Geometry,"
reprinted from *Reports of a Mathematical
Colloquium*, (Notre Dame, Ind., 1948), p. 2;
F. Klein, *Vorlesungen ueber Nicht-Euklid-
ische Geometrie* (Berlin, 1928), p. 171; R.
Courant and H. Robbins, *What Is Mathematics?* (New York, 1941), pp. 220-221.

127. Klein, *op. cit.*, pp. 146-153; Courant and
Robbins, *op. cit.*, pp. 224-226.

128. A. Cayley, *Collected Works* (Cambridge,
1889) II, 561-592; F. Klein, *Gesammelte
Mathematische Abhandlungen* (Berlin,
1921), I, 254-305; II, 311-343.

129. O. Veblen and J. Young, *Projective
Geometry* (Boston, 1918), II, 171 ff.

130. Science is being defined here in the strict
sense of the *Posterior Analytics*.

131. *In IV Phys., op. cit.*, 6, nn. 6-8.

132. Heath, *op. cit.*, I, 154.

Published by the Marquette University Press
Milwaukee, Wisconsin 53233
United States of America

1 St. Thomas and the Life of Learning (1937)
 by John F. McCormick, S.J.

ISBN 0-87462-101-1

2 St. Thomas and the Gentiles (1938)
 by Mortimer J. Adler, Ph.D.

ISBN 0-87462-102-X

3 St. Thomas and the Greeks (1939)
 by Anton C. Pegis, Ph.D.

ISBN 0-87462-103-8

4 The Nature and Functions of Authority (1940)
 by Yves Simon, Ph.D.

ISBN 0-87462-104-6

5 St. Thomas and Analogy (1941)
 by Gerald B. Phelan, Ph.D.

ISBN 0-87462-105-4

6 St. Thomas and the Problem of Evil (1942)
 by Jacques Maritain, Ph.D

ISBN 0-87462-106-2

7 Humanism and Theology (1943)
 by Werner Jaeger, Ph.D., Litt.D.

ISBN 0-87462-107-0

8 The Nature and Origins of Scientism (1944)
 by John Wellmuth

ISBN 0-87462-108-9

9 Cicero in the Courtroom of St. Thomas Aquinas
 (1945) by E. K. Rand, Ph.D., Litt.D., LL.D.

ISBN 0-87462-109-7

#10 St. Thomas and Epistemology (1946)
 by Louis-Marie Regis, O.P., Th.L., Ph.D.

ISBN 0-87462-110-0

#23 Thomas and the Physics of 1958:
A Confrontation (1958)
by Henry Margenau, Ph.D.

ISBN 0-87462-123-2

#24 Metaphysics and Ideology (1959)
by Wm. Oliver Martin, Ph.D.

ISBN 0-87462-124-0

#25 Language, Truth and Poetry (1960)
by Victor M. Hamm, Ph.D.

ISBN 0-87462-125-9

#26 Metaphysics and Historicity (1961)
by Emil L. Fackenheim, Ph.D.

ISBN 0-87462-126-7

#27 The Lure of Wisdom (1962)
by James D. Collins, Ph.D.

ISBN 0-87462-127-5

#28 Religion and Art (1963)
by Paul Weiss, Ph.D.

ISBN 0-87462-128-3

#29 St. Thomas and Philosophy (1964)
by Anton C. Pegis, Ph.D.

ISBN 0-87462-129-1

#30 The University in Process (1965)
by John O. Riedl, Ph.D.

ISBN 0-87462-130-5

#31 The Pragmatic Meaning of God (1966)
by Robert O. Johann

ISBN 0-87462-131-3

#32 Religion and Empiricism (1967)
by John E. Smith, Ph.D.

ISBN 0-87462-132-1

#33 The Subject (1968)
by Bernard Lonergan S.J., S.T.D.

ISBN 0-87462-133-X

#34 Beyond Trinity (1969)
by Bernard J. Cooke, S.J., S.T.D.

ISBN 0-87462-134-8

#46 The Gift: Creation (1982)
   by Kenneth L. Schmitz, Ph.D.
                              ISBN 0-87462-149-6

#47 How Philosophy Begins (1983)
   by Beatrice H. Zedler, Ph.D.
                              ISBN 0-87462-151-8

#48 The Reality of the Historical Past (1984)
   by Paul Ricoeur
                              ISBN 0-87462-152-6

#49 Human Ends and Human Actions (1985)
   by Alan Donagan
                              ISBN 0-87462-153-4

#50 Imagination and Metaphysics in St. Augustine
   (1986) by Robert J. O'Connell, S.J.
                              ISBN 0-87462-227-1

#51 Expectations of Immortality in Late Antiquity
   (1987) by A. Hilary Armstrong
                              ISBN 0-87462-154-2

#52 The Self
   (1988) by Anthony Kenny
                              ISBN 0-87462-155-0

#53 The Nature of Philosophical Inquiry
   (1989) by Quentin P. Lauer, S.J.
                              ISBN 0-87462-156-9

Uniform format, cover and binding.

Copies of this Aquinas Lecture and the others in the series are obtainable from:

Marquette University Press
Marquette University
Milwaukee, Wisconsin 53233, U.S.A.

Publishers of:
• Mediaeval   • Père Marquette   • St. Thomas
  Philosophical   Theology Lectures   Aquinas Lectures
  Texts in Translations